Puzzle Dinosaurs

Susannah Leigh

Illustrated by Brenda Haw

Contents

Edited by Jenny Tyler
Design co-ordinator: Laura Parker

About this book

This book is about Abby and Isaac and their amazing dinosaur discovery. There are puzzles to solve on every double page. If you get stuck, you can look at the answers on pages 31 and 32.

Abby and Isaac are staying by the sea. A fierce storm has washed up lots of interesting things onto the beach, and Abby and Isaac investigate.

They spot a big rock, imprinted with a strange creature. Isaac is sure they have found a fossil. Excitedly, he takes a photo with his new camera.

Isaac

Abby

Interesting Things You Might Find In A Rock Pool:

shells

crab

Fossil – part of a dead plant or animal that has been buried and turned as hard as stone by chemicals in the rock.

fossil

Things to spot

Abby and Isaac don't know it yet, but they are about to go on an amazing dinosaur adventure. See if you can spot one of these prehistoric things on every double page.

big blue rat

dragonfly

flying frog

gingko tree

tortoise

newt

star-tailed snake

amber

ammonite

giant blue claw

Stegoceras

prehistoric sea otter

ghost shark

Dinosaur teeth

Look out for dinosaur teeth. There is one tooth to spot on every double page.

Morgan the Morganacudon

This prehistoric creature is a Morganacudon. His name is Morgan. See if you can spot him on every double page.

3

Dinosaur clues

That night, Abby and Isaac lay listening to the sound of the waves crashing onto the shore. Another storm was brewing. Outside, the moon cast its light over the fossil on the beach.

Abby took a closer look at the photo Isaac had taken earlier.

"I'm sure this is a dinosaur fossil," she said. "It has a long, pointy tail and short front legs. Is there anything like that in your dinosaur book, Isaac?"

Can you help Isaac identify the fossilized dinosaur?

dinosaurs from the late Cretaceous period.

MEAT EATERS

Troodon:
Long tailed.
Liked to eat
Maiasaurus!

T Rex:
Big and bad.
The daddy of
the dinosaurs!

Deinonychus:
This dinosaur
was built to kill!

PLANT EATERS

Edmontosaurus:
A large duck-
billed dinosaur.

Achelousaurus:
A plant eater
with a parrot-
like beak.

Maiasaura:
It had a long,
pointy tail and
back legs bigger
than its front legs.

Parasaurolophus:
Plant eater with
a pointy tail.

www.usborne.com

Deadly bees lived in these beehives

A prehistoric poisonous snake

5

Stormy skies

Just then, a flash of lightning struck the fossil and a blinding light filled the room. When the light faded, Isaac and Abby found themselves back on the beach. The tide was rolling in. On a rock in the middle of the deep water was a familiar-looking creature.

"It's a dinosaur!" Isaac cried. "A Maiasaura, just like the fossil we found. Except this one's alive."

"And stranded on that rock," Abby pointed. "I think I can see a way to lead it to safety before the tide comes in."

Can you find a safe way across the sandbanks and rocks to reach the little dinosaur?

Back in time

Isaac and Abby scrambled safely across to the Maiasaura. The dinosaur looked surprised to see them, but the children were even more surprised when it actually spoke to them.

"I've lost my parents and I'm stuck on this rock!" it wailed.

"Don't worry," Abby said kindly as they led the dinosaur to the safety of the shore. "We'll help you."

Isaac was trying to make sense of everything. "This Maiasaura must have come alive in our time," he said.

My name's Maya.

I'm Abby. This is Isaac.

"Or else," he continued, spotting
something very scary in the bushes.
"We've somehow gone back to the
time of the dinosaurs. Look out!"

What has Isaac spotted?

Run for your life!

Crashing through the trees came a terrifying, giant dinosaur.

"It's a meat eater!" cried Maya. "Run for your lives!"

Isaac and Abby didn't need to be told twice. One blast of hot breath from the prehistoric monster was enough to make them sprint for cover.

Abby dived into a bush.

Maya found a hollow log.

Isaac ran.

The meat eater chased him.

Isaac reached a tree...

...and climbed up. The meat eater shook the tree with his mighty claws. Isaac thought he would fall. Then, just when he thought things couldn't get any worse, he saw another type of meat-eating dinosaur – and then some more.

Can you spot the other five meat-eating dinosaurs?

Looking for Dad

Isaac closed his eyes. He thought this was it. Then he heard Abby shout, "Quick, climb down."

Isaac opened his eyes. The meat eaters were all attacking each other! Isaac grabbed his chance and raced down to join Abby and Maya in the bushes.

"Let's get out of here before they spot us again," whispered Abby.

This is your print, Maya.

The trio ran quickly. They came to a clearing. Here, lots of strange tracks led off in different directions in the ground.

"Some of these look like your paw prints, only bigger," Abby said to Maya.

"They might be my parents' prints," Maya said excitedly. "My dad's are easy to spot. He's missing part of a toe. He lost it in a fight."

Can you spot Maya's dad's prints here?

13

Helping Maya

As the ground became drier, the prints stopped. Then, Isaac spotted them again in the muddy earth on the other side of a mountainous maze.

"Should we go any further?" Abby whispered to Isaac. "How will we get home again?"

"I don't know," he replied. "But we can't leave Maya here by herself."

"Yes, you're right," said Abby. "We should find her parents. Let's go."

"Hey, wait," Isaac said. "I think those long-necked creatures are Ornithomimus. They can be fierce and fast when they're awake."

"Those long-nosed things are nasty too," added Maya. "We'd better step carefully and quietly."

Can you find a safe way to the prints, avoiding the Ornithomimus, and the long-nosed creatures?

Stampede!

Safely through the twisty maze, Maya soon spotted her dad's prints again. They set off on the trail.

"Um, what's that noise?" Isaac said, hearing a faint drumming sound. "It's getting closer."

"Dinosaurs!" cried Abby.

A herd of stampeding dinosaurs raced towards them, trampling everything in their path. It was time to get out of the way – and fast.

Can you find them a safe, empty hiding place from the stampeding dinosaurs? Do you know what type of dinosaurs these are?

Lava trouble

Maya peered out from their hiding place.
"All the creatures I can see here are friendly," she said.
"They were just stampeding because they were scared.
And I know why. Look!" She pointed to an erupting
volcano, noisily spouting out fire and ash.

"The friendly creatures are hiding now," said Maya.

BEFORE

"Is it safe to go out?" asked Abby.

"Not yet," Isaac warned. "I can see a rather frightening creature. And what's more, I think it can fly."

What has Isaac seen? Where have the friendly creatures hidden?

AFTER

Flower power

Isaac pointed up at the sky. A group of mean-eyed flying reptiles came screeching overhead, their pointed beaks poised to attack.

Isaac drew back his outstretched arm, but it was too late. One of the flapping monsters had scratched him on the arm with its razor-sharp claws.

The giant creatures swooped back for a second attack.

"Run for it," cried Abby.

They ran to take cover in a nearby forest.

"I think we lost them," Abby panted. "How's your arm, Isaac?"

Isaac looked miserable. "Badly scratched," he said.

Maya took a look. "Don't worry. I know a beautiful orange flower with pink leaves that will soothe that," she said.

"I can see it!" said Abby.

Can you spot the soothing orange flower?

21

Swamp lizards

Isaac rubbed his arm with the soothing leaves.

"That's much better," he smiled.

"At least it's cooler away from that volcano," said Abby.

They rounded a corner and found they were staring at an enormous swamp.

"I can see my dad's prints on the other side." exclaimed Maya. "We have to get across, but we'd better be careful. Dangerous giant lizards live in this swamp."

Isaac spotted a fallen tree trunk and Abby grabbed some branches. "We can paddle across on this log," they grinned. "Come on!"

Can you find a safe way through the swamp? Look out for the giant lizards!

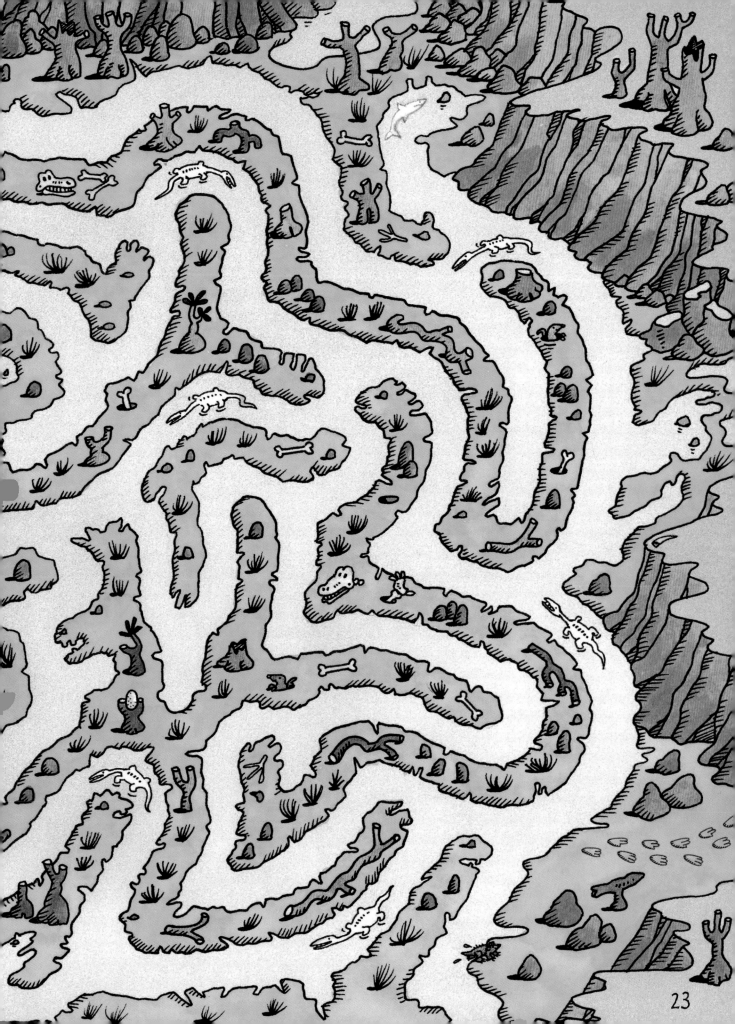

Sneaking past snakes

They jumped off the log, ran down a path and bumped straight into a huge dinosaur. Isaac was about to turn and flee, when Maya let out an excited yell.

"It's my friend, Al."

"Maya," Al whispered. "Where have you been? We've all been worried. And what are those strange creatures with you?"

"They're not strange," Maya said. "They're Abby and Isaac. I was lost and they rescued me. Why are we whispering, Al?"

"Because the trees here are full of poisonous snakes," hissed Al. "There are deadly beehives too. Climb onto my back. I'll sneak quietly past and take you to your parents. But you will have to help me look out for the dangerous creatures."

Can you spot the snakes? There are ten of them. There are four deadly beehives too.

25

Dinosaur Valley

Quietly and carefully, Al crept off into the jungle, away from the snakes. Then, around a corner was the most amazing sight. A mighty herd of dinosaurs grazed by a lake. Isaac thought he recognized some of them from his dinosaur book.

Suddenly Maya gave a cry of excitement. "My parents!"

Can you spot Maya's parents? How many other types of dinosaur do you think Isaac can recognize?

"Morgy!"

Lightning strikes twice

Maya's parents were overjoyed to see her. "We heard the meat eaters coming and we called to you to run," her dad explained. "But you had wandered away from us, Maya and we couldn't find you. We thought we'd never see you again."

"I'm safe now, thanks to my new friends Abby and Isaac," Maya smiled.

As they talked, dark clouds appeared overhead and the wind began to blow. A flash of lightning filled the sky, and in that moment the dinosaurs disappeared. Abby and Isaac found themselves back in the beach house. Isaac's dinosaur book was still on the bed. The fossil was still outside the window. Or was it?

What has happened to the fossil?

Back home

The next morning, Abby and Isaac were back on the beach, but they couldn't stop thinking about their amazing dinosaur adventure.

"Maya isn't a fossil anymore," Isaac said, looking at the empty stone. "So I guess when we went back in time, we must have saved her life."

"I'm glad she's with her parents again," Abby sighed. "But I'm going to miss her."

"Me too," agreed Isaac. He reached into his bag for his camera, to take a picture of the space where Maya had been. "Hey, I almost forgot," he said, pulling out something round. "I picked up this interesting rock on our adventure. Look."

"Isaac, that isn't a rock. It's a dinosaur egg!" Abby cried. "And I think it's about to hatch!"

Look back through the book. Can you spot a dinosaur egg on each double page?

Answers

pages 4-5

The fossilized dinosaur is a Maiasaura.

pages 6-7

pages 8-9

Isaac has spotted a giant dinosaur!

pages 10-11

pages 12-13

These are Maya's dad's prints.

pages 14-15

pages 16-17

The stampeding dinosaurs are Parasaurolophus.

pages 18-19

pages 20-21

pages 22-23

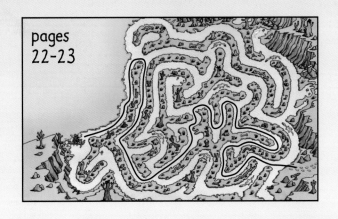

pages 24-25

pages 26-27

Here are Maya's parents.

Some of the other dinosaurs here are Parasaurolophus, Achelousaurus, Edmontosaurus.
(You saw them in Isaac's dinosaur book on page 4.)

pages 28-29

The stone is empty and the fossilized Maya has disappeared.

page 30

Did you spot the dinosaur eggs? (There isn't one on pages 2 and 3).

Did you spot everything?

Did you spot Morgan the Morganacudon on every double page?

And did you find the dinosaur teeth?

First published in 2007 by Usborne Publishing Ltd., Usborne House, 83-85 Saffron Hill, London EC1N 8RT, England. www.usborne.com Copyright © 2007 Usborne Publishing Ltd.

The name Usborne and the devices are Trade Marks of Usborne Publishing Ltd. All rights reserved. No part of this publication may be reproduced, stored in a retrieval system or transmitted in any form or by any means, electronic, mechanical, photocopying, recording or otherwise, without the prior permission of the publisher.

First published in America 2007 U.E. Printed in China.

The list shows you where the things to spot are hidden.